D1582130

ANDREW CARNEGIE

A Life from Beginning to End

Copyright © 2018 by Hourly History.

Table of Contents

Introduction

Andrew Carnegie was born to William Carnegie and Margaret Morrison Carnegie in the sleepy Scottish village of Dunfermline on November 25, 1835. To say that the home that he was born into was a modest one would be a great understatement. Known as a "weaver's cottage," it was equipped with only one room that was made up of half the ground floor, which was shared with the neighboring weaver's family.

In these meager and modest surroundings, the child named Andrew Carnegie would dream of his future. He imagined himself to someday be important and play a great role in society. Even at a young age, he began to think of how he could help lift his family out of the dire straits that they had found themselves in. His mother was always a shining light on his course of self-sacrifice, and just as she herself always put others before her, she expected Andrew to learn to do the same.

Andrew Carnegie would indeed eventually help to carry the weight of his burdened family over the next few decades. The family would stay ensconced within the humble confines of their weaver's cottage until the year 1836 when they moved to a bigger house on Edgar Street just across from the famous Reid's Park in Scotland. It was here that Andrew's uncle George Lauder, an up-and-coming political agitator in the British Empire, began to take young Andrew under his wing and teach him the ropes of his political intrigue.

Despite their poverty, many members of Andrew's family were politically active. His maternal grandfather Thomas Morrison, for example, was a known Chartist—those who believed Scotland should be given a "people's charter" or basic bill of rights—in the region. But beyond the periodic delvings and dabblings into the political scene of the day, life went on rather uneventfully in the Carnegie family until Andrew was about the age of 12 and his father's business as a handloom weaver began to hit the rocks.

But it wasn't just his father's business that was in peril, at this point in time all of Scotland was in a bit of a crisis, and the whole country was being threatened with starvation on a massive scale. During these hard times, the only way that the family survived was through the efforts of Andrew's mother, who began to run a small grocery store out of their home. She also began to work as a cobbler making shoes—a skill that she had learned as a child from her father who practiced the same trade. It was through all of these efforts that Mrs. Carnegie became the primary breadwinner of the family.

And while this certainly provided much-needed relief to the struggling Carnegies, it was a hard blow to the esteem of Andrew's father who saw himself as the family provider. But nevertheless, it was through Margaret's savings that they managed to scrape together enough money to buy a ticket out of their misery. Soon they would be on board a ship headed to a land that promised greater opportunity than the stagnant confines of their homeland. The Carnegies were headed to America.

Chapter One

The Life of a Scottish Bobbin Boy

"The average person puts only 25% of his energy and ability into his work. The world takes off its hat to those who put in more than 50% of their capacity, and stands on its head for those few and far between souls who devote 100%."

—Andrew Carnegie

By 1848, the Carnegie family were so fed up with the fate that Dunfermline, Scotland offered them that they began to pack their bags to board the next ship to the United States of America. Margaret's two sisters, who had already made the move to America, encouraged the family's decision. But not all of their relatives in Scotland were happy about such talk, however, and some considered their plans to drop everything and run to the U.S. as being reckless. Tom Morrison, Margaret's brother, would go even further, calling the family's actions nothing short of treacherous and idiotic.

Morrison, of course, was an unrelenting Chartist ideologue and wished his family to stay in Scotland to fight for Chartist rights rather than jumping ship and abandoning the cause. And the Chartist fervor was indeed heating up, as evidenced in April of 1848 when a Chartist Convention organized a mass meeting with the aim of presenting a petition to Parliament. The demonstration was peaceful, not anything like the 1842 petition that ended in outright strikes and riots. In August of 1842, a huge crowd of disgruntled workers—men, women, and children—all took to the streets with brooms, sticks, and whatever other blunt object they could muster with the intention of wreaking havoc upon the very factories, storehouses, and shops that they worked for.

And for once, it was actually the firebrand Tom Morrison that urged the enraged throng to cease their attack. He threw himself headlong into the thick of the chaos, imploring the rampaging protestors to stop destroying property and instead organize a peaceful general strike. His efforts were noble, but they were apparently in vain, and the fact that he was trying to take control of the situation only earned him recognition as a ringleader. That perception motivated the police to knock on the door of the Carnegie home to have a talk with Tom Morrison—a speaking engagement that resulted in Morrison being placed in jail.

As this back and forth struggle between the authorities and the Chartists continued to play out, by 1847 unemployment in the region hit rock bottom, eventually leading to food riots in the Scottish cities of Glasgow and Edinburgh. In these dire conditions, the Carnegies finally made up their mind to leave Scotland for good. They raised money by selling all of their belongings, and with little else with them but their hopes and dreams, they set sail from a port in Glasgow for the long-awaited promise of the United States in 1848. The trip wasn't easy and would take them across 4,000 some miles of treacherous ocean current, and not all passengers would survive.

Indeed, as shocking as it may seem today, more than a few passengers succumbed to sickness and disease during the voyage before they ever arrived at their intended destination. Out of simple necessity, with nowhere to bury or store the dead, the ship captain ordered the grieving families to push their dead overboard and bury them at sea. This was the harsh reality of Carnegies' world in which one often had to make great sacrifices for the sake of survival.

Shortly after arriving in America, the Carnegie family made their way over to the town of Allegheny, Pennsylvania. Allegheny at that time was a center of major industry which produced many products involving cotton cloth and wool. Allegheny made so many products that it became common for articles of clothing to have the label "Made in Allegheny."

But as much as they were in the heart of heavy industry, Andrew's father William did not see any immediate improvement in his employment as a weaver. He found it hard to find companies willing to sell his wares (often tablecloths), and he was not having any luck selling them on an individual level either. Upon their arrival, the family's financial sustenance had been once again placed upon the shoulders of Andrew's mother.

While her husband still struggled to find a steady job, Margaret had managed to gain work for a cobbler, binding shoes together. She earned four dollars a week for her labors, which was a substantial amount for the struggling—near destitute—family. This was a godsend, but it certainly wasn't easy for Andrew's father to sit on the sidelines. His fortunes would soon look up, however, as both he and his son Andrew found work for a Scotsman, Mr. Blackstock, at the Anchor Cotton Mills.

The labor at this mill was hard, but it was a boost to the family's confidence all the same. Little Andrew was given the job of a bobbin boy, tasked with changing spools of cotton thread. He typically did this no less than twelve hours a day and for six days out of any given week. His pay for his labors amounted to just $1.20 a week, which is about $35 by today's standards. It was a fairly meager income even back in 1848. Such a task couldn't have been easy for a 13-year-old, and in later years child labor of this sort would ultimately be banned, but as it were, Andrew Carnegie persevered and did his best under the circumstances that he had been given.

Many immigrants who arrived in America during the 1840s would settle for less than what their native-born competitors made just to have a good solid job, and this was the case with the Carnegie family as well. Although his father would soon quit his position at the cotton mill, Andrew would stay on for some time to come. Diligent and dutiful, young Carnegie continued to plug away and give it all he had, disregarding the fact that his position was a lowly one, "I was now a helper to the family, a breadwinner, and no longer a total charge on my parents." His efforts soon earned him recognition from a big-name manufacturer named John Hay. Hay was impressed with Andrew's hard work and offered him a job and a raise in the amount of $2.00 per week, which would be about $58 today. It was definitely a step up for the poor immigrant laborer.

The work at Hay's factory was loathsome. Carnegie was tasked with bathing brand new spools in special preservative oil. He would later recall that the hardest thing about this job was having to put up with the constant odor of the overpowering oil. As Carnegie described it, "Not all the resolution I could muster nor all the indignation I felt at my own weakness, prevented my stomach from behaving in almost perverse way. I never succeeded in overcoming the nausea produced by the smell of oil. But if I had to lose breakfast or dinner, I had all the better appetite for supper, and the allotted work was done."

No longer accompanied by his father, Andrew was now left to walk to and from his job in the factory by himself. But he wasn't alone for long, and soon he would meet the acquaintance of a few young men whom he would be friends with for life. Calling themselves the "Original Six," this group of working-class youth consisted of Carnegie, John Phipps, William Crowley, Thomas Miller, James R. Wilson, and James Smith. This group made it a part of their regular routine to meet up on their only day off—every Sunday—so that they could discuss all of the latest political intrigue and current events of their time. Although tasked with menial jobs, all of these young men were ambitious just like Carnegie, and it was second nature for them to debate such complex topics at great length.

It was together with his young friends that Carnegie made the efforts that cold winter of 1848-1849 to better himself by attending night classes in Pittsburgh where he was taught a valuable new skill, double-entry bookkeeping. Carnegie would not, however, be given the chance to revolutionize Mr. Hay's accounting practices as he had planned. Because before the year 1849 was out, he was offered a job as a telegraph messenger boy at an office of the Atlantic and Ohio Telegraph Company located in Pittsburgh, Pennsylvania. This job paid him $2.50 a week—about $75 today—for his efforts. Right away Carnegie showed himself to be a very industrious team member and had managed to commit all of the regular service locales to his memory. Along with this gift of memorization, Andrew Carnegie also seemed to have the uncanny ability of mimicry and interpretation. He could hear just about any click or sound of the telegraph and recognize it by ear and then reproduce it verbatim.

As he continued to excel in his work at the telegraph company, Carnegie also began to pursue academic studies when a man by the name of Colonel James Anderson, at his own expense, opened up his personal library consisting of some 400 different texts in order for working boys to achieve their own self-styled education. This is where Carnegie was truly able to further his education. Carnegie would always be thankful for this library of information that he had been gifted, and one day he would repay the world with countless libraries and educational foundations that would bear his own name.

Chapter Two

Carnegie Enters the Railroad Business

"The man who acquires the ability to take full possession of his own mind may take possession of anything else to which he is justly entitled."

—Andrew Carnegie

As a young man, Andrew Carnegie's first big break in life came on February 1, 1853 when he was given gainful employment for the Pennsylvania Railroad Company. He was handpicked by the superintendent of the rail company, a man by the name of Thomas A. Scott. The Pennsylvania Railroad had just installed a series of telegraph lines and needed an ambitious new telegraph operator—Scott saw that ambition in young Andrew Carnegie. He immediately appointed Carnegie to the post as well as the job of being his personal secretary. Here Carnegie was given his best paycheck yet, and he was truly excited to work for the railroad as he saw it as an industry in which there was endless opportunity for continued growth and development. And as always, Carnegie's greatest competitor was himself, setting self-imposed standards to which he would push himself to follow.

The only thing that troubled 17-year-old Carnegie about his new position was the fact that it brought him contact with the operating crews—the "rough men" whom he often referred to as being "crude and vulgar." These hard-working laborers were apparently at the bottom of the barrel of the working class in those days, and their antics were frequently bawdy enough to make Andrew Carnegie cringe. Full of profanity, drunkenness, and obscene humor, these men often grated on Carnegie's more refined nerves, "This was a different world, indeed, from that to which I had been accustomed. I was not happy about it. I ate, necessarily, of the fruit of the tree of knowledge of good and evil for the first time."

But for young Carnegie, it was a small price to pay for the privilege that he had been granted. He valued every moment of his work, viewing every shipment and bill of lading that he processed as a learning experience. He was able to learn quite a bit about the real world of business through the materials that made daily transfers across his desk.

Everything was going well enough for the young man at first, but then one day during a business trip to the town of Hollidaysburg, Carnegie almost made a fatal mistake. He had been holding close to his person a bundle of payroll checks during the trip—crucial articles for any operation—when at some point during the course of the journey they had slipped from his person and fell down onto the tracks. When Carnegie realized his mistake, he was desperate to get the checks back and pleaded with the engineer to reverse the train so he could take a look at where the bundle of checks may have dropped off. Fortunately for Carnegie, as the train reversed course, his desperate eyes were indeed able to make out the brown paper bag that contained the lost payroll documents.

Not wasting any time, or even thinking one second for his own safety, Carnegie leaped from the moving train and lunged at the package, yanking it from its precarious position just off of a river bank, snatching it up before it fell into the water below. Andrew Carnegie would come to remember this mishap for many years. Even though in the end he was able to successfully recover the lost payroll checks, he knew how close he had come to devasting failure, a failure that could have meant the end of his career.

Carnegie would later reflect that this incident had served to humble him, and he would always remember it, lest he judged others too harshly for their errors and honest mistakes. As he would later describe it, "I have never since believed in being too hard on a young man, even if he does commit a dreadful mistake or two; and I have always tried in judging such to remember the difference it would have made in my own career but for an accident which restored to me that lost package at the edge of the stream a few miles from Hollidaysburg."

But even so, if Carnegie deemed that those underneath him were negligent and derelict in their duties, he did not hesitate to exact punishment upon them, as was proven just a few months after the Hollidaysburg incident when Scott had relinquished supervisory powers to the young Carnegie during a week when he was out of town. An accident had occurred on the tracks, and Carnegie found it was due to the direct bungling of the ballast crew. He was determined to punish the miscreants for the deed.

Carnegie did so by delivering what he referred to as his "court-martial." He stopped all operations and investigated the accident to the utmost; at the end of his investigation, he determined to fire one of the men responsible and suspend another pair of men whom he deemed to be part of the problem. This was Carnegie's first real taste of authority, and in hindsight, he lamented that he had not shown more leniency, "Some of these [men] appealed to Mr. Scott for a reopening of the case, but this I never could have agreed to, had it been pressed. More by look I think than by word Mr. Scott understood my feelings upon this delicate point and acquiesced. It is probable he was afraid I had been too severe and very likely he was correct. . . . I had felt qualms of conscience about my action in this, my first court."

His next chance to take the initiative came shortly thereafter, when one morning while his boss was again out of the office. Carnegie was alone at the desk when he received an urgent message that one of the trains had been in an accident, and the other freight trains were backed up as a result. Carnegie immediately sought out his superior officer, but unable to find him, he took matters into his own hands. He knew the train tracks like the back of his hand at this point, and he knew exactly what to tell the engineers to do. So, he gave them instructions by telegraph signing off on the message with the initials of his boss, Mr. Scott.

Upon his superior's return, Carnegie was at first fearful that perhaps he had gone too far, but he would later hear it through the grapevine of the railroad that his boss was quite pleased with his actions. Scott felt that young Carnegie's decision to take control was bold and perhaps a bit brash, but he was deeply impressed by the determination and sheer expertise that he exhibited in doing so. With such strong wind in his billowing sails, it seemed that absolutely nothing could stop the rise of Andrew Carnegie.

Chapter Three

The Pittsburgh Promotion

"The problem of our age is the proper administration of wealth, so that the ties of brotherhood may still bind together the rich and poor in harmonious relationship."

—Andrew Carnegie

As successful as Carnegie's professional life had been, tragedy would strike his personal life when on October 2, 1855 his father William Carnegie, aged 51, passed away from a long and protracted illness. Even before the death of his father, Andrew had been the primary source of income for his family. As such, he would continue to work hard and excel at his work for the railroad company.

It was also during this time that Carnegie made his first investment. The opportunity presented itself to Carnegie when he was informed by Scott that a man named William Reynolds had just passed. As it turns out, the ten shares that Reynolds had owned in the Adams Express Company, which had been left to his widow, were now being sold at a relatively cheap price. Carnegie was informed that he could get in on the venture for as little as $600.

Scott told his young protege that this would be a tremendous investment and even offered to help him raise the sum if necessary. But as the story goes, his mother, who had been such a vigorous force and often served as the sole provider for her family in the past, came through for Andrew Carnegie once again. Carnegie would later say that it was his mother who had raised the money for him by mortgaging their home. If such accounts are to be believed, this would seem to be quite a touching story. But more recent research into the life of Carnegie would discover a red herring that seemed to point to a bit of fabrication on the part of Andrew Carnegie and his later biographers, in regard to how he managed to obtain this piece of stock. It would later be discovered that Carnegie had left an IOU note for $610 in his preserved paperwork, addressed to none other than his boss Thomas Scott, conspicuously dated May 17, 1856—the very date that he is said to have purchased the stock.

This evidence has largely proven Carnegie's later telling to be a fictitious account, but there is some truth to his version of the story. To be able to pay back Scott, Carnegie eventually borrowed money from a George Smith, and in the spring of 1858, his mother agreed to mortgage their house in Allegheny to secure the funds to pay off the loan.

Shortly after the stock purchase, Scott was promoted to the position of general superintendent and was set to move to the central office in Altoona in late 1856. Carnegie, his loyal assistant, followed him there to work as his secretary at a salary of $50 a month. Initially the two men even shared accommodation, most likely because Scott was grieved by the recent loss of his wife. Carnegie later wrote of the situation, "At his desire I occupied the same large bedroom with him. He seemed anxious always to have me near him."

One evening Carnegie was walking home from the office when he realized someone was stepping close behind. Alarmed, he turned around and was approached by a man who worked for the railroad. The man said that Carnegie had helped him in the past to land his blacksmith job, and he now wanted to repay the favor. The man then divulged to Carnegie confidential information he had that the railroad workers were planning a general strike. Armed with this foreknowledge,

Carnegie then quickly went on to inform his boss, Mr. Scott, what was afoot. As a result, all the names of the would-be strike leaders were quickly posted, and all those involved were fired from their jobs.

The partnership of Andrew Carnegie and Thomas Scott would continue unabated until 1859 when Carnegie's world on the rails was rocked by the news that the vice president of the railroad company, William B. Foster, had abruptly passed away. As a result, Scott was immediately recommended to take his place. The idea of losing the boss with whom he had such cordial relations over the past few years filled Andrew Carnegie with a sense of dread. He simply couldn't entertain the idea of working under anyone else and was concerned by the fact that Scott would be leaving.

But after Scott returned from his interview and confirmed his hiring for the position, he had an extra bit of news for Carnegie as well. He informed his assistant that since the shakeup of Foster's passing, the former superintendent of the Pittsburgh division, Mr. Potts, was promoted to the transportation department in Philadelphia. This meant that there was a new role to be filled for superintendent of the Pittsburgh division, and Scott had been asking around if Carnegie could fill that role. Scott was then pleased to inform Carnegie that the folks back at the Pittsburgh division had heartily agreed to give Andrew Carnegie a chance in the newly opened position. They were extending the young man an opportunity of a lifetime, and he would never forget it.

Carnegie was elated to hear the news, and with a starting salary of $1,500 a year, he signed onto the position on December 1, 1859. From the lowly bobbin boy of yesteryear to becoming the superintendent of his own railroad at the age of 24, Andrew Carnegie had come a long way. The promotion he received in Pittsburgh would forever change the trajectory of his life, and just like the powerful steam engines he presided over, once Carnegie's train was on the track, it was full steam ahead—there was no looking back.

Chapter Four

Carnegie During the Civil War

"Do your duty and a little more and the future will take care of itself."

—Andrew Carnegie

In what could be described as perhaps his first action of nepotism, as soon as Carnegie was assigned the role of superintendent of the Pittsburgh division, he made sure that he hired on his now 16-year-old brother Tom as a telegrapher and his own personal secretary. He had also moved his family back to the city of

Pittsburgh, putting them up in a home in a busy, downtown, working-class neighborhood.

The area was bristling with industry, and according to Carnegie's later recollection the industrial activity of the nearby factories was so intense that he said in part, "If you placed your hand on the balustrade of the stair it came away black . . . The soot gathered in the hair and irritated the skin . . . life was more or less miserable." There were glass factories and textile mills on every corner, but the most important industry of the city was the production of steel.

Before the football team ever existed, this was the true heyday of the Pittsburgh Steelers—this was steel town in all of its glory. For the most part, Carnegie's time directing the Pittsburgh division went well enough, he already knew the ropes and knew how to lead. The only real problem he encountered as he began his work was the incidence of railroad workers who did not take him seriously enough because of his age and youthful appearance. During one exchange for example, when Carnegie was apparently absentmindedly standing in the way of one of his subordinates, the worker, a big strapping Irishman, screamed at him, "Get out of me way, ye brat of a boy!" The laborer's hostility was only taken down a notch or two when some of his co-workers explained to him that Carnegie was his boss. But even with his personal relations squared away on the railroad, there was soon enough intrigue on the international level to go around.

In 1860, shortly after the election of Abraham Lincoln, several states in the south who opposed Lincoln's views on slavery decided to secede from the Union. Lincoln had championed an eventual abolition of the practice, and for staunch supporters of abolition such as Andrew Carnegie, Lincoln's election served as a vindication of their beliefs in a free and just society despite the turmoil it provoked in the southern half of the country

On February 14, 1861 when Lincoln visited Pittsburgh on the way to his inauguration, most in Pittsburgh were ecstatic and full of support for their new president. Just a few months later this excitement would be tempered, however, when on April 12, the states that had already voted to secede crystallized their votes with bullets by firing upon Fort Sumter in Charleston, South Carolina. Carnegie's telegraph lines were very busy that day as desperate citizens sought to learn more about the latest happenings in the aftermath of the hostilities.

Fort Sumter ultimately surrendered to the bombardment it faced on April 13, prompting Abraham Lincoln to proclaim that local militias should be formed. It was in response to this that the city of Pittsburgh formed a Committee of Public Safety. Headed by a man who was Carnegie's own neighbor, this committee commenced to gather as many local volunteers and as much equipment as it possibly could in order to support the—as of yet still undeclared—war effort.

Carnegie for his part, soon found himself overwhelmed with all of the people and materials traveling through his rail station. Along with monitoring these developments, he was also tasked with the job of making sure that no supplies were secretly shipped from northern collaborators to the southern Confederates. The situation soon grew even worse when word came that Confederate agents had tampered with railroad tracks in Baltimore and cut the telegraph wires. From there, enemy activity progressed from sabotage to open attack when four Union troops were shot and killed. The door to Maryland was then slammed into the face of the Union when the governor decided to join the Confederates, expelled all federal troops, and ordered all bridges and railroads to be shut down. The Union, of course, was not going to take such things lying down and quickly initiated a strategic response of its own.

As a result, Andrew Carnegie found himself in the middle of the chaos, being ordered to Annapolis, Maryland to serve on a team tasked with reconstituting the sabotaged rail lines. The best they could do under the conditions was to take a train down to the shoreline of Chesapeake Bay. From here they boarded a steamer in the company of Union soldiers of the

Sixth Massachusetts Regiment. Upon their arrival, Carnegie's team got to work making sure that the railroad and telegraph lines between Annapolis and Washington, D.C. stayed open.

Although he did not see any combat during this dangerous mission, Carnegie would receive a grievous wound. He later describes how he was in the process of unfurling a telegraph line when it abruptly sprang back up and hit him right across the face, leaving a deep cut right in the side of his cheek. After stopping the flow of blood, Carnegie proceeded with the rest of the train headed to Washington, D.C. as planned.

Carnegie was reportedly proud of his battle scar and would later recall the feeling that, though he wasn't in uniform, he did indeed shed his blood for the nation. Once this successful sortie had ended, Carnegie then proceeded work to extend the rail and telegraph lines from downtown Washington all the way to Alexandria.

It was from this vantage point that the Union troops planned to take the fight to the Confederates. Carnegie's job entailed setting up miles of track and rebuilding Long Bridge, and it was through these new channels that Carnegie directed the transport of wounded soldiers. At that point in time hundreds had already been killed, and several hundred more had been wounded.

Carnegie would then soon receive word that the Confederate army was closing in on his own position and was forced to flee on the very last train to Alexandria just as what would be known in the annals of the Civil War as the Battle of Bull Run was about to begin in earnest. Andrew Carnegie was not a soldier, and he was most definitely not looking for war, but the call of battle had certainly found him.

Chapter Five
Return to Scotland

"Think of yourself as on the threshold of unparalleled success. A whole, clear glorious life lies before you. Achieve! Achieve!"

—Andrew Carnegie

Carnegie returned to Pittsburgh during the last summer months of 1861 where he once again oversaw the transport of troops and munitions from the eastern seaboard to the front lines. Although he himself was safe from the physical threat of war, the grueling schedule of his vocation took a toll on him all the same. Coupled with his ill health, right around this time Carnegie had to face the stress of his former boss and long-time adviser, Thomas Scott, being accused of price gouging.

Charges had been leveled that Scott was not charging fair prices to the federal government for services—something that the officials did not take lightly and which soon led to an official congressional investigation. Andrew Carnegie received such news in great distress and alarm, not only because of the fate that might be in store for his former mentor but also out of fear over what might happen to him as Scott's loyal assistant.

Carnegie was implicated by virtue of the fact that he was the point man and had kept the books during these supposed times of financial indiscretion. The investigation soon passed, however, and more good news arrived to replace the bad. This time, the good word came in the form of petroleum deposits that were discovered just 60 miles north of Pittsburgh. In what amounted to nothing short of an oil rush, Carnegie's contemporaries seized upon the findings in a frenzied determination to make themselves rich.

When Carnegie arrived on the scene, he was amazed at what he discovered. He found a gathering of the most provocative of clientele. There were now bars, casinos, and brothels on just about every corner. The area become so notorious in fact that it developed quite a name for itself—taken right out of the pages of the Holy Bible's description of depravity personified—locals jokingly referred to it as "Sodden and Gomorrah." But despite all of the decadence, the spot was indeed productive when it came to oil. By

1862, it was host to numerous flowing oil wells. Carnegie was pleased to have leaped at the opportunity, having bought for himself stocks at $10 apiece.

The next major milestone to occur in Carnegie's life was in June of 1862 when he took a leave of absence and boarded a boat for Scotland. Taking with him his mother as well as his friend and associate Thomas Miller, Carnegie was determined to go on an adventure and retrace the steps of his childhood. The ship set sail on June 28 and arrived at the port of Liverpool two weeks later. From here Carnegie and his group of fellow sightseers traveled by train across the border to Scotland and to the open arms of the family that he had long left behind.

Here Carnegie was amazed to discover that his memories from childhood now appeared quite different than the reality he saw on the ground. The shops and stores he remembered passing through as a child now seemed like nothing more than antiquated hovels, "Everything seemed so small, compared to what I had imagined." Nevertheless, he made the most of his stay, regaling his family with tales of America, stories of the war, and endlessly debating the politics and intrigue of the day.

Somewhere in the midst of this heated discourse, however, Carnegie came down with a severe fever and was forced to be confined to bed. The treatment that he was given didn't make him much better; he was subjected to the ancient art of bleeding, in which it had been determined that just about any illness known to man could be treated by the shedding of a little blood. The bloodletting was almost the end of Carnegie, however, as his treatment seemed only to exacerbate his illness. Fortunately, he persevered and was able to set sail back for America in the fall of 1862.

Chapter Six
Building His Empire

"While the law [of competition] may be sometimes hard for the individual, it is best for the race, because it insures the survival of the fittest in every department."

—Andrew Carnegie

As the Civil War heated up, Andrew Carnegie made what would be his last major wartime investment. In the spring of 1864, he and his close friend Thomas Miller acquired a five-acre plot of farmland from which they removed a series of half-grown cabbages in order to make room for their newly manufactured steel mill. In October their firm was officially put into business. They named the outfit the Cyclops Iron Works in an homage to the Cyclops of Greek mythology who had been known to devour men.

Carnegie's new investment was threatened with interruption, however, when he received an unexpected draft notice in the summer of 1864. Andrew was under the belief that the draft board would not call his number since under the recently enacted Conscription Act of 1863, it had been stated that all train engineers and other essential personnel would not be included in the draft. To his great disappointment, the draft board had apparently not deemed his vocation as superintendent to be crucial enough.

Carnegie soon found a loophole out of his dilemma. In those days it was custom for those who did not wish to fight to avoid the draft by hiring an alternative. So, Carnegie contacted an agent who found him a suitable alternative in the form of an Irish immigrant named John Lindow. It was through this arrangement that Carnegie received his Certificate of Non-Liability on July 19, 1864. Saved from the draft, Carnegie then sought to figure out what his next career path would be and soon he came to the conclusion that he wished to leave the railroad business. Drafting his resignation on March 28, 1865, he wanted to become a speculative investor full time. He now began to place all of his efforts into the steel mills fulltime.

But although he had officially left the railroad, Carnegie would continue to keep close tabs on what was happening through his continued contacts with his old boss Thomas A. Scott and chief engineer J. Edgar Thomson. It was also through the close ties he had with these former associates that he managed to enter into yet another lucrative venture, which he came to call his Keystone Bridge Company.

This enterprise actually had begun during the Civil War when Carnegie had partnered with a man by the name of Colonel John L. Piper and a bridge builder named Aaron Shiffler. Bridges had been in desperate need during and after the war since the Confederates and their sympathizers had destroyed many viable bridges—especially steel bridges needed for trains. Initially the firm had been known as the Piper and Shiffler Company, but after the war Carnegie had reorganized and renamed it the Keystone Bridge Company. This was done in honor of Pennsylvania which was known as the Keystone State.

The Keystone Bridge Company was officially incorporated on May 16, 1865 with the capital of $200,000 behind it. The first major project was then underway in late 1868 with plans to build what would become the Keokuk-Hamilton Bridge, spanning across the Mississippi River, in between Iowa and Illinois. This giant bridge would end up being a length of no less than 2,300 feet. The next major contract for the Keystone Bridge Company to take on was the building of the Eads Bridge in St. Louis. This iconic bridge was completed and opened to the public in 1874. Building bridges were proving to be quite a lucrative business venture for Andrew Carnegie, but not as lucrative as his burgeoning steel empire would soon become.

Throughout the 1870s, Carnegie began to focus his attention as an investor on the steel industry, and his keen eye for business helped him come out from the depression caused by the Panic of 1873 virtually unscathed. Thomas Scott, his former mentor and boss, was not as lucky. Scott went to his old protégé for help after the crash left him in a financial crisis. Carnegie refused, however, and their friendship quickly ended after that.

It was right around this time period that Carnegie began to really make his mark on the steel and iron industry. His innovative use of the Bessemer process, in which steel is produced quickly and efficiently in a special Bessemer converter that heats the molten steel at a slight tilt to speed up the process, allowed Carnegie to bring mass-produced, quality steel to the United States and the world at large. In 1883, Carnegie was able to buy out one of his major competitors, the Homestead Steel Works.

Then in the fall of 1883, with such great dividends from his business dealings, Carnegie sought another great venture by asking his long-time girlfriend Louise Whitfield to marry him. At just 26 years old, she presented a formidable age gap for the now middle-aged industrialist, but as with everything else in his life, Carnegie was determined to make it work.

As it turned out, the biggest obstacle the union was presented was his mother who showed her disapproval of the marriage prospect from the beginning. Most mothers would probably be happy to have their son—especially one that had been single as long as Carnegie—get married. But this was just not the case with Margaret. Carnegie had been the sole support for his aging mother for several years now, and she seemed to be morose to share this support system with anyone else. It was for this reason that Carnegie determined to put off his marriage to Louise until after his mother's passing. After what at times felt like a morbid kind of vigil, Andrew Carnegie's mother then passed away on November 10, 1886.

Even though he and his bride-to-be were almost anticipating the event, Carnegie was devastated all the same. Overcome with grief, he didn't even speak to Louise until six weeks later. The two did not marry until the next year, on April 22, 1887. The 51-year-old bachelor finally married his 30-year-old bride and thereby left his old life as the single industrialist behind in favor of starting a family of his own.

Chapter Seven

The Gospel of Wealth

"Surplus wealth is a sacred trust which its possessor is bound to administer in his lifetime for the good of the community."

—Andrew Carnegie

Andrew Carnegie would continue his rise up the industrial ladder, and by the late 1880s, he had gained quite a monopoly over steel and pig iron. It is said that by the year 1889, U.S. production of steel surpassed all of England's production, and within that assortment it was Andrew Carnegie who owned more than his fair share.

Along with these advances in business Carnegie also began to implement what he came to call his "Gospel of Wealth" in which he donated his time and money seeing to the cultural enrichment of the community. This was the case in November of 1895 when he took a train back to Pittsburgh to kick off his 60th birthday by opening one of his famed Carnegie libraries. The library was officially dedicated on November 5 in the Music Hall of the building. Following a speech given by a local

Episcopalian priest, Carnegie spoke to the excited crowd of onlookers.

He explained to those in attendance how he planned to give back much of the wealth he had gained. He told them that "surplus wealth must sometimes flow into the hands of the few," in what he termed to be a "sacred trust, to be administered during life by its possessor for the best good of my fellow men." And Andrew Carnegie did not disappoint, donating millions of dollars to the building of libraries, museums, and technical institutions. All of these efforts served to leave an indelible legacy for Mr. Carnegie, not only in the city of

Pittsburgh but the rest of the world for years to come.

Carnegie meanwhile had accumulated more wealth in his personal life when his wife Louise gave birth to Margaret, a daughter named after Andrew's mother, on March 30, 1897. With his family life set and his businesses generating more money than he could spend, by 1901, Carnegie was so rich and successful that he considered retiring. With this idea in mind, he had placed much of his assets into a joint stock package.

Helping him to organize his retirement savings was none other than John

Pierpont Morgan, the famed banker and financial wizard of the era. Morgan knew that Andrew Carnegie himself was a shrewd and successful businessman, so he was determined to cut him the retirement deal of a lifetime. Morgan believed that the best way to go about doing so was to purchase Carnegie's holdings as well as the holdings of others and consolidate them all under one massive company in order to streamline the process.

It was these efforts that produced the United States Steel Corporation on March 2, 1901. Right at the dawn of the twentieth century, U.S. Steel would become the richest corporation in the world, exceeding the billion-dollar mark. And at this point, Carnegie was one of the wealthiest people in the world, a fact that motivated him to move toward another stage in his life—one of philanthropy. This included the establishment of libraries and generous donations to charitable organizations all over the world. Carnegie also began to engage in peace talks on a global scale, attempting to avert war and conflict at any cost. It is said that Carnegie would give an estimated 21 million in the year 1903 alone. Carnegie was also a member of the Anti-Imperialism League, a group of activists determined to stem the tide of imperial ambition abroad.

But along with all of this activism and charitable ambition, 1903 was also a year of personal tragedy when Carnegie's friend and mentor Herbert Spencer passed away. Spencer was part railway engineer, part philosopher, and Andrew Carnegie loved everything the man said. Often referring to him in letters as "master," Carnegie truly saw the man as a sage of great wisdom, sparing him no great question. In December 1903 when while Spencer was on his deathbed, Carnegie is said to have asked him one of the biggest questions of all, inquiring of him, "Why must we die?" Spencer, the master philosopher, sadly did not have the answers that Carnegie was looking for and passed away on December 8, unable to render a successful treatise on the subject.

As he became increasingly aware of his own mortality, Carnegie would come to ask this same question more and more. But even though he was pondering his future demise, in the early 1900s the old man was still just as robust in his sixties as he was in his forties. And the spring and summer of 1904 would come and go like any other, with the elder Carnegie living it up at his vacation home in Scotland with his wife and daughter in tow. Here Carnegie would wake up to bagpipes and breakfast, as he attempted to keep his mind on anything but the steady march of time.

Chapter Eight

False Claims and Fraud

"I shall argue that strong men, conversely, know when to compromise and that all principles can be compromised to serve a greater principle."

—Andrew Carnegie

The idyllic peace of Andrew Carnegie's later years would be disturbed in late 1904 by a woman who claimed to be his illegitimate daughter. The instance occurred when a certain Cassie Chadwick in Cleveland, Ohio had convinced her husband, who was a doctor, and all of his acquaintances that she was indeed the daughter of Andrew Carnegie and could tap into the mainline of Carnegie's wealth. Her scheme was so convincing that bankers in the area offered her large loans, totaling between $10 and $20 million, on the assumption that Andrew Carnegie would be there to take care of the debts and repay the money.

When it became clear that Mrs. Chadwick could not repay her substantial loans, a summons was given to Andrew Carnegie who was suddenly placed into the position of having to prove that he was not the deceptive woman's long-lost father. Carnegie made a brief court appearance in March 1905 and left shortly thereafter. In the end it was discovered that Chadwick was delusional, suffering from mental illness, and prone to making up outlandish stories. This sad, deranged figure was certainly a headline maker for the early twentieth-century press, and soon the gossip columns were abounding with extra salacious and sensational details of Cassie Chadwick's story. Some even suggested that she had run a brothel back in Cleveland, where she was said to have kept "immoral resorts" that trafficked in young women and "almost every crime in the criminal catalogue."

While these stories are typically viewed as nothing short of tabloid sensationalism, Chadwick did indeed have a long history of fraudulent activity that can be documented. As a young lady in 1878 for example, it is said that she had concocted a bizarre scheme in which she attempted to change her identity in order to fence valuables. She apparently had her long hair chopped off and had a fake mustache glued to her face before attempting to hawk a gold watch. Those around her at the time felt that young Chadwick was not in her right mind, and although the police were called, taking her skewed mental state into consideration, they did not press charges and simply escorted the troubled woman home.

This leniency and understanding did not help matters though, and from here Chadwick's strange games of deception would only continue. Since she had gotten away with it once, she apparently figured she could get away with it again and began to embark upon a veritable career of writing bad checks. In the same fashion that ensnared Carnegie, she would weave wild webs of deceit connecting herself to wealthy men, claim their patronage, and then fraudulently sign their names on promissory notes. Chadwick's history of fraud only ceased when she was sentenced to 14 years in prison for her crimes. Here she sadly passed away in 1907, ending the last chapter of a very troubled life.

Andrew Carnegie meanwhile had encountered even more personal problems, this time due to his very real daughter, Margaret, who in late 1905 fell off of a swing and sustained an injury to her leg. The exact nature of the injury was unclear; initially those who looked at it believed that she was merely suffering from a sprained ankle. But when she did not immediately show signs of recovery, she was seen by a specialist who removed her ankle cast and replaced it with a cast for her entire leg. Margaret would continue to have trouble with her legs, however, and from age eight to eleven she would be in constant need of crutches.

Her father would continue his philanthropic work, and in the spring of 1906, Carnegie would attend the celebration of the Silver Jubilee of the Tuskegee Institute, which had been founded in Tuskegee, Alabama by famed African-American entrepreneur Booker T. Washington. Carnegie was an avid supporter of the initiative that Booker T. Washington had started, annually donating funds to the institution.

In early 1907, Carnegie attended the international Hague Conference. Just a few years before, in 1903, he had contributed about $1.5 million for the construction of the Hague's famed Peace Palace. The second Hague Peace Conference started on June 15, 1907, but to Carnegie's chagrin the peace efforts ultimately failed to produce any meaningful results. It was this failure that led to Carnegie's call for the establishment of a League of Peace and then for the much more famous League of Nations. Carnegie even wrote an article for *Outlook* magazine on May 25, with the title "The Next Step—a League of Nations."

It seemed that Carnegie was destined to be a great visionary not only in the world of steel and iron but also in the world of peace. And toward these efforts he made yet another generous contribution to the cause in the form of the Carnegie Endowment for International Peace in 1910. According to Carnegie, he believed that these efforts were going to serve to "hasten the abolition of international war." Carnegie was a tireless advocate of this cause in the next few years, but sadly, all of these efforts could not seem to stave off the war to end all wars, World War I.

Chapter Nine

World War I Peace Efforts

"Perhaps the most tragic thing about mankind is that we are all dreaming about some magical garden over the horizon, instead of enjoying the roses that are right outside today."

—Andrew Carnegie

The year 1914, on the very eve of World War I, Andrew Carnegie was trying his best to stave off the inevitable. The first sparks of the war had already been ignited when a disgruntled Serbian nationalist decided to assassinate the archduke of Austria, Franz Ferdinand. This murder then led to the inevitable crisis produced by the international entanglement of the era which saw the formation of two opposed factions—those supporting the Austrians and those allied against them—squaring off in a catastrophic global showdown.

It was precisely the thing that Andrew Carnegie was actively attempting to avoid with his talk of forming a League of Nations that could talk out any tensions or ill will before it led to horrific war. As a last-ditch effort for peace, Carnegie attempted to place himself as the international go-between of the major world powers, as a final effort at remediation. In pursuing these efforts, Carnegie soon came to believe that personally convincing the Kaiser to cease hostilities was the true key to averting the crisis.

Some have even come to claim that Carnegie offered to bribe the Kaiser with several million dollars to get him to agree to back down. But whatever the case may be, the efforts made to beseech the Kaiser ultimately failed, and the war proceeded in full force as scheduled. The disappointment in the current state of events was clarified in a message sent from Robert Franks to Andrew Carnegie's secretary that read in part, "The war news is terrible and shocking. I do feel so sorry for Mr. C. after having peace so close to his grasp."

Until this point, Andrew Carnegie had started to retire more and more to his retreat in the Scottish countryside, his idyllic Skibo Castle. This gem of the Scottish Highlands was his escape, but upon hearing the news of the outbreak of war, Carnegie decided to travel to America; he would never return to his homeland again. His birthday that November was a rather sad affair as well. He invited reporters to his library for a conversation, as was his usual birthday routine, but Carnegie admitted to them that the war had shaken his "proverbial optimism about the goodness of the world."

Just as Robert Franks' message had suggested, Andrew Carnegie was indeed quite inconsolable as the war he had tried so hard to prevent completely engulfed Europe. Suffering from anxiety attacks and feelings of great depression, Carnegie was now as it were desperate for his third act in life. He was already a great businessman and philanthropist, but he had tried and failed to be a peacemaker; he now needed a third rail on which he could place all of his unbridled ambition.

It wouldn't be until around the time of his 82nd birthday that Carnegie would receive the birthday gift that he wanted—an end to the war to end all wars. On November 11, 1918, World War I was finally over, at the cost of just over 16 million lives. Andrew Carnegie could only hope and pray that the tragedy of the Great War would not be repeated. In that sense it could be said that it is rather fortunate that Mr. Carnegie would not live to see the rise of Fascism that led the globe down the road to World War II.

Andrew Carnegie was a dreamer, and he yearned for a world in which his dreams could be fulfilled. He felt that he had been blessed with a great surplus of wealth and that it had been placed upon his shoulders to use it for the betterment of humankind. But sadly, all of the libraries, art museums, and philanthropic trusts he could muster were never quite enough to completely enlighten the dark heart of man and bring about the peaceful brotherhood Andrew Carnegie so desired.

Conclusion

Andrew Carnegie passed out of this world on August 11, 1919, just a few months shy of his 84th birthday. He spent his last day on Earth at his personal estate in Lenox, Massachusetts. The official verdict as to the reason for his demise was listed as a bad case of bronchial pneumonia. Immediately after his passing, his family was inundated with a swarm of letters and telegrams of consolation.

The world had lost a great man who had given much of his money and time trying to make it a better place. Carnegie had already given away more than $350 million (about $77 billion today), and immediately after his passing, a prearranged installment of an additional $30 million was sent off to his charities and philanthropic trusts. After his funeral, Carnegie's last place of rest was chosen to be at Sleepy Hollow Cemetery in Sleepy Hollow, New York. Andrew Carnegie was gone, but he most certainly was not forgotten.

His name lives on in the countless libraries, art museums, schools, charities, and all-around good causes that he promoted both during his life and after it came to an end. They say that Andrew Carnegie is the father of the philanthropist—the modern-day concept of the wealthy giver. Always ascribing to his "Gospel of Wealth" which urged those who had a surplus to spread their wealth to the masses, Andrew Carnegie would certainly be pleased to know that his name and legacy continues to stir that very same sentiment of benevolence and good will for others, just as he intended.

Printed in Poland
by Amazon Fulfillment
Poland Sp. z o.o., Wrocław
27 March 2023

cbbfa166-533c-4f48-92a8-3666b3d5ae67R01